Thomas Birch's Sons

Catalogue of Exquisite Examples in Still Life

Being Oil Paintings by the late William Michael Harnett

Thomas Birch's Sons

Catalogue of Exquisite Examples in Still Life
Being Oil Paintings by the late William Michael Harnett

ISBN/EAN: 9783337053789

Printed in Europe, USA, Canada, Australia, Japan

Cover: Foto ©ninafisch / pixelio.de

More available books at **www.hansebooks.com**

THE

WM. MICHAEL HARNETT COLLECTION

HIS OWN RESERVED PAINTINGS

MODELS AND STUDIO FURNISHINGS

NOW ON EXHIBITION IN OUR ART SALESROOM

SECOND FLOOR

SALE CONDUCTED BY

No. 27.

EXECUTRIX'S SALE

CATALOGUE

—OF—

EXQUISITE EXAMPLES IN
STILL LIFE

BEING

OIL PAINTINGS

By the Late William Michael Harnett

INCLUDING

THE FURNISHINGS OF HIS STUDIO

Embracing: A Magnificent **Carved Ivory** Crucifix; Antique
China; Bronzes **and Brass Ornaments**; Draperies
Models, Books, etc., etc., etc.

ALSO

A GENUINE CREMONA VIOLIN

AND

HIS PENCIL AND CRAYON SKETCHES

TO BE SOLD

IN OUR ART SALESROOM, SECOND FLOOR

THURSDAY & FRIDAY EVENINGS, FEB. 23 & 24, 1893

COMMENCING AT 8 O'CLOCK

SALE CONDUCTED BY

STAN V. HENKELS

THOMAS BIRCH'S SONS
Auctioneers
1110 CHESTNUT STREET   PHILA.

NOW ON EXHIBITION

WILLIAM MICHAEL HARNETT was born in Clona-
kilty, County Cork, Ireland, August, 10, 1848, and was
brought to America when but a year old. He was
educated at St. Mary's Parochial School, and at Zane Street
Grammar School. When but thirteen years old, he sketched
his first picture on a slate, while at the above school. To quote
the artist: "My first picture was not painted, neither was it
drawn with crayon, nor sketched with India ink, but with a
slate-pencil, on a slate." This slate, which is in the sale, was
found, after the death of his mother, among her effects.

His farther died in Philadelphia when William was a small
boy, and he was obliged to do something to help support his
mother and his small sisters. His first work was selling news-
papers, after which he served as an errand boy. When seventeen
years old he began to learn the engraver's trade, and worked on
steel, copper and wood, and finally developed considerable skill
in engraving silverware; but the introduction of plated ware,
which is engraved by machinery, caused Mr. Harnett to abandon
his trade.

From his early youth he showed great talent in drawing, and
at the age of nineteen, he entered the night class at the Pennsyl-
vania Academy of the Fine Arts as a pupil. Two years later he entered the night class of the National Academy of Design and the
Cooper Institute of New York, meanwhile following his trade as
an engraver during the day, working for some of the largest
jewelry firms in New York. In 1875 he gave up this trade
and devoted his entire time to painting, studying under Thomas
Jensen, for a short time.

One of his first compositions in oil was a pipe and a German beer mug; it was exhibited at the New York Academy and
sold for $50.00. This was the first money he earned with his
brush. In 1876 he returned to Philadelphia, and opened a studio;
he then exhibited in the Academy of the Fine Arts, and be-
came a member of the Society of Artists. Soon after this a con-
noisseur, from Munich, bought one of his productions. This was
the first example of his work to cross the water. It was here
that his larger and more noted pictures were produced, among
which were—"After a Hard Night's Study," "Front Face," "A
Job Lot," "The Professor's Table" and "Confusion." These
passed into the hands of collectors as soon as finished.

In 1878 Mr. Harnett went to London and remained there

several months, where he painted pictures, which were sold, and he also exhibited in the National Academy of London.

From there he went to Frankfort and then to Munich which, was his home for four years. Afterwards he visited a number of places in Germany, collecting his stock of models and antiquities from noted collectors and art museums.

In October of 1884 he went to Paris, remaining there one year; it was there he painted his famous picture "After the Hunt," which he sent to the Salon and it was accepted. M. Louis Enault, the famous French critic, who annually publishes a book, in which he gives reproductions of forty paintings from the current Salon, included this picture among those he chose for that year. At the close of the exhibition he returned to New York with his triumph of art, and opened a studio in that city. Here he painted his well-known pictures, namely, "The Old Cupboard," "Music," "The Old Violin," and others.

At this time Mr. Harnett painted a "Five Dollar Bill," for Theodore Stewart, of New York. After delivering it, news of its existence reached the Secret Service Bureau, of the Treasury Department, at Washington, whose agents seized it. The picture was sent to Washington, and, when examined by an expert, was pronounced to be merely a painting in oil. The late Judge McClue, solicitor of the Treasury, decided that it was a work of art and not a counterfeit, and could not be confiscated. It was then restored to the owner, but Mr. Harnett was warned by the Secret Service authorities not to indulge his fancy in that direction again. Mr. Harnett always grouped his models so as to make an artistic composition.—he endeavored to make the composition tell a story; before painting the objects he would make a finished lead-pencil drawing, with minute details.

Mr. Harnett through hard study and years of toil achieved for himself the highest fame in his line of painting, being recognized as the most realistic painter of this age. For many years he had been a great sufferer from rheumatism; he visited Carlsbad and the Hot Springs, of Arkansas, but found only temporary relief. He died at the New York Hospital, October 29, 1892, after a short illness, as only three days before he was at work in his studio, where he was found unconscious. The funeral services were held in this city at St. Augustine's Church, Fourth and New streets. Solemn Requiem Mass was celebrated, after which the interment was at Cathedral Cemetery.

E. TAYLOR SNOW.

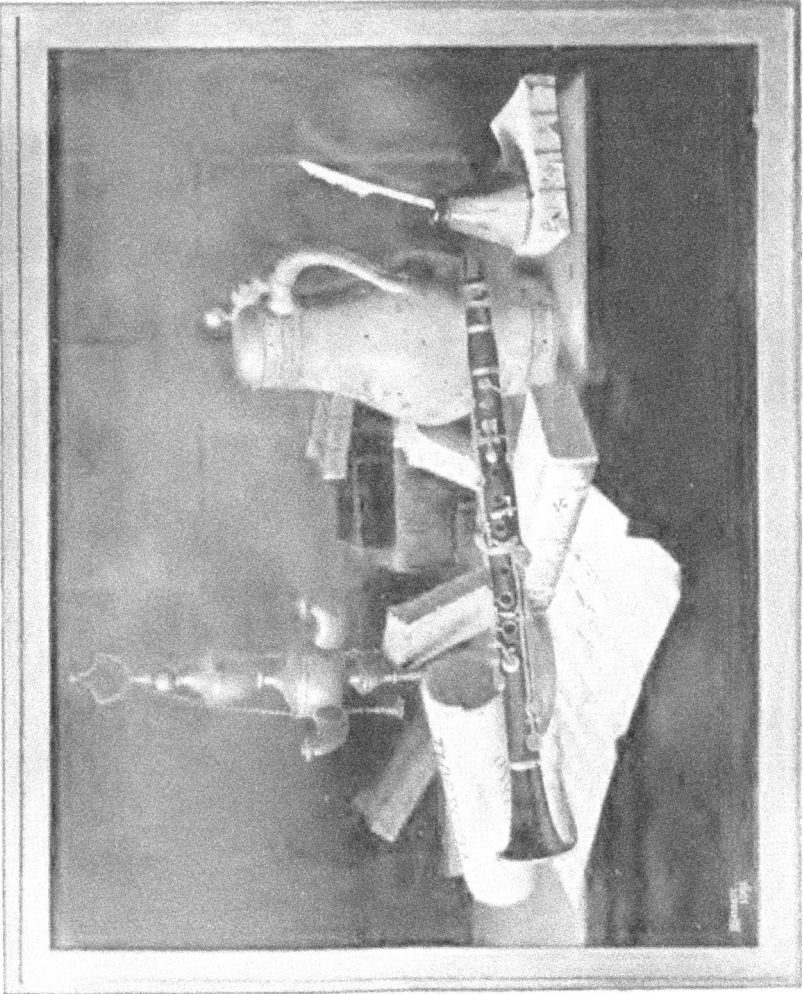

No. 5.

CATALOGUE

1 LEAD PENCIL DRAWING
   Roman soldier's head

2 PENCIL DRAWING
   Monogram " W. M. H."

3 PENCIL SKETCH
   Still life

4 PENCIL SKETCH
   Still life

5 PENCIL SKETCH
   Still life

6 PENCIL DRAWING
   Horse's head

7 PENCIL DRAWING
   Pattern for a spoon

8 PENCIL DRAWING
   Pattern for a spoon

9 OIL PAINTING
   Old head

10 CRAYON DRAWING
   Bust of Augustus

11 CRAYON DRAWING
   Roman head

12 CRAYON DRAWING
   Roman head

13 CRAYON DRAWING
Bust of Julius Brutus

14 CRAYON DRAWING
Bust of Julius Cæsar

15 CRAYON DRAWING
From the antique

16 CRAYON DRAWING
Portion of a head

17 COLORED DRAWING
Club monogram

18 INK DRAWING
Design for chandelier

19 LARGE CRAYON DRAWING
Gladiator

20 CRAYON DRAWING
Minerva

21 CRAYON DRAWING
Cupid

22 LARGE DESIGN IN COLORS
" Vermachlung der Helena." By W. Forndran

23 CRAYON DRAWING
Old head

24 CRAYON DRAWING
Julius Cæsar

25 CRAYON DRAWING
Female head. Drawn at Munich, 1881. Framed and glazed

26 CRAYON DRAWING
Old man's head. Drawn at Munich, 1862. Framed and glazed

No. 29.

MR. HARNETT'S OWN RESERVED PAINTINGS.

27 ★OLD MODELS   Painted 1892

This grand production is the last effort of Mr. Harnett; was painted
for the Chicago Exposition. The articles delineated in the painting
are faithfully depicted in the photographic reproduction which illus-
trates this catalogue, and the articles themselves will be found at this
sale.

This painting is considered his masterpiece, and, in realism, sur-
passes all other productions.

28 ★PROFESSOR'S OLD FRIENDS   Painted 1891

This beautiful and realistic masterpiece was the next to the last painting
that emanated from his easel. For objects included in the grouping,
see reproduction. The technique is most marvelous—the brass, is
brass; and the wood, is wood.

29 ★ REMINISCENCES OF OLDEN TIME
                              Painted, Munich, 1880

This is the first painting in which he included ancient armor. It
was painted at Munich, for the exhibition of 1880, and there exhibited.
Mr. Harnett was awarded the greatest praise by all the art connoisseurs
of that art centre for the wonderful realistic effect portrayed on this
canvas.

30 ★ YE KNIGHTS OF OLD   Painted at Munich, 1880

This wonderful painting was exhibited at the Munich Exhibition of
1880. We need say no more in its praise than to mention that the
artists of Munich decorated this painting with flowers. See reproduction.

31 SIDE SPRING LAMB   Painted at Munich, 1882

This was the last picture exhibited at Munich. It is said that this
painting was the cause of a serious accident, which damaged many of
the beautiful models which had been collected by Mr. Harnett. Whilst
putting the finishing touches upon it a gentleman friend called upon
him, accompanied by a large mastiff, which, being persuaded that the
leg of lamb was genuine, made one grand rush for—a good dinner;
this upset the easel, which fell against the table on which were the
models; and hence the accident.

32 BUNCH OF ASPARAGUS   Painted 1890, at New York

Faithfully depicting a prize bunch of asparagus raised by a gentleman friend of his in Harlem.

33 A FAITHFUL COLT — Painted 1890

A genuine old Gettysburg relic. If the canvas could hold a nail we would say that the revolver itself was only hung on it. See the newspaper remarks attached to the painting.

34 COLOSSAL LUCK — Painted 1886

An English dray horseshoe, rough and rusty, as just taken from the street where found, carrying good luck to the possessor.

34a A BACHELOR'S FRIEND — Painted 1880

A realistic grouping of just the objects one would expect to find on a table in a bachelor's studio.

35 WILD DUCK

An unfinished picture, which Mr. Harnett was painting to order for a resident of St. Louis, for which he was to receive $5000.

36 OLD BOOKS

An unfinished canvas.

37 OIL PAINTING

Old Master.
Portrait of Raphael.

ARMOR.

38 OLD SWORD

Very rare, carved ivory handle, brass mounting and painted by Mr. Harnett, in his celebrated pictures, "After the Hunt," "Confusion" and "Bric-a-brac."

39 ∗ RARE OLD GUN

Ancient fire-lock of the fifteenth century; very heavy and curiously carved stock, rifled barrel, fine steel mountings; one of the finest models owned by Mr. Harnett, and painted by him in his famous picture, "After the Hunt"; procured at a great expense from a collection at Stuttgart.

40 ∗ COMBINATION SHOTGUN AND RIFLE

Very choice piece, beautifully carved wood stock, representing a deer, in action. This gun was introduced by Mr. Harnett in his exhibition picture, at Munich, 1883. The picture was sold from the exhibition to the celebrated art collector, Adolph Loewi, of Regensburg.

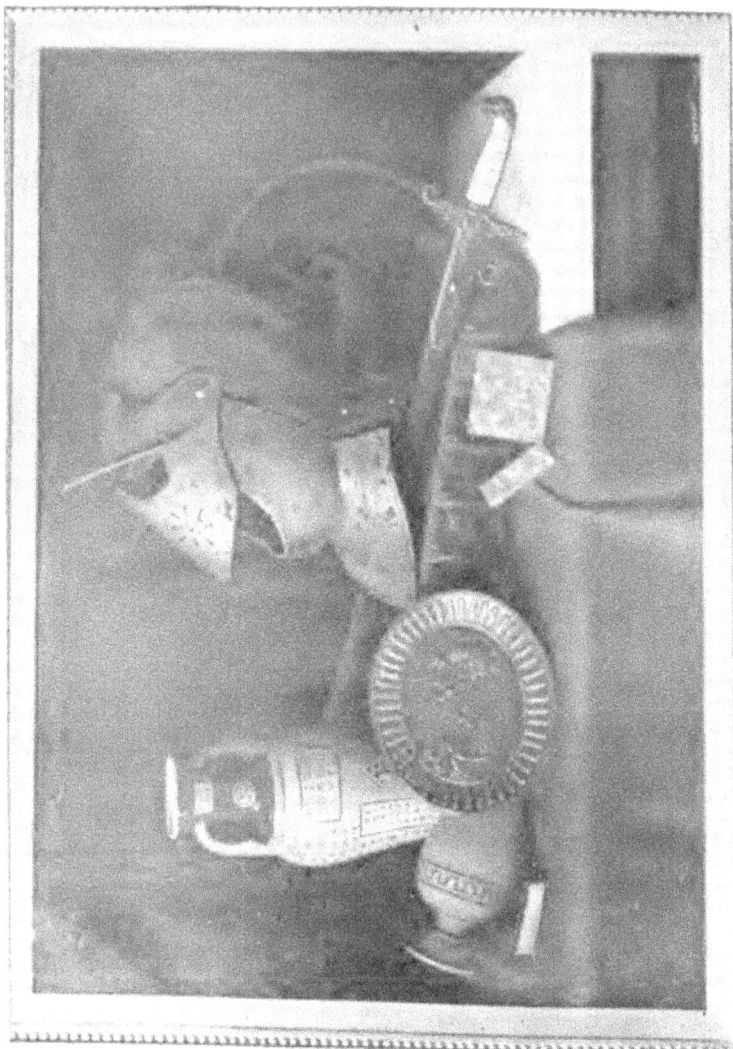

No. 20.

41* FLINT-LOCK PISTOL.

The stock, mounted with a silver-plated parrot's head, brass mount ings, and copied by Mr. Harnett in several of his paintings.

42* HORSE PISTOL.

Used in the War of 1812.

Farragut Coll. 91 43* COLT'S REVOLVER

Made famous by Mr. Harnett's realistic painting of the same

44 STEEL HELMET

Old and rare; purchased in London from a famous collector; painted by Mr. Harnett in several of his most famous pictures.

45* HUNTER'S HORN

Black horn with gilt mountings, purchased in Munich

46* HUNTER'S HORN

Brass horn, with bone mouth-piece

47* POWDER HORN

48 * POWDER HORN

Antique, flat, mounted with brass, from a noted Düsseldorf collection

after Hunt 65 49 OLD POWDER HORN

A relic of the Revolution, painted in "After the Hunt," and other compositions

" 50 ANTIQUE BRASS HUNTER'S HORN

Painted in Mr. Harnett's famous picture "After the Hunt," which was exhibited in the Paris Salon; it is now a great attraction in the Stewart collection in New York. Being considered one of the most realistic grouping of hanging objects he ever painted

51 COPPER POWDER FLASK

52 HUNTING KNIFE

Antique carved tusk handle

53* HUNTING KNIFE

Buckhorn handle, silver-mounted

54* HUNTING KNIFE

Antique bone handle, brass mounting

55 PAPER KNIFE, SILVER PLATED

Dolphin's head

MUSICAL INSTRUMENTS.

55½* CREMONA VIOLIN

(Old model)
1894
the Life of Violin?
old Cremona, 1895

Rare old violin. "Joseph Guarnerius, fecit. Cremona, anno 1724, I H S." A remarkable sweet-toned instrument, procured by Mr. Harnett at a great cost from a celebrated collection in Paris. It is introduced into several of his pictures, including his last painting

56* ROMAN MANDOLIN

Antique. A feature of several of Mr. Harnett's famous pictures sold in Europe

Iris Life of Viol. 86
The Old Violin 94

57* OLD VIOLIN

Painted in the compositions of "Old Cupboard Door," "Artist's Table," "Music," and other noted pictures

58 SMALL TAMBOURINE

59 LARGE TAMBOURINE

Painted in the "Old Cupboard Door," owned by William B. Bement, of Philadelphia

60* EBONY CLARIONET

Silver-plated keys, classed in several of Mr. Harnett's most noted pictures

61* CLARIONET

Amber colored, grouped in the painting which was exhibited in the New York Academy, 1886, and purchased by a noted collector in the West

Professor's Old Friends 1891

62* EBONY FLUTE

Ivory mouth piece; silver-plated keys. Mr. Harnett's oldest model, painted in his first large canvas, "After a Hard Night's Study," considered one of his best groupings. Owned by a collector in this city

63 BRASS CORNET

Copied by Mr. Harnett in several of his groupings

64* GERMAN-SILVER CORNET

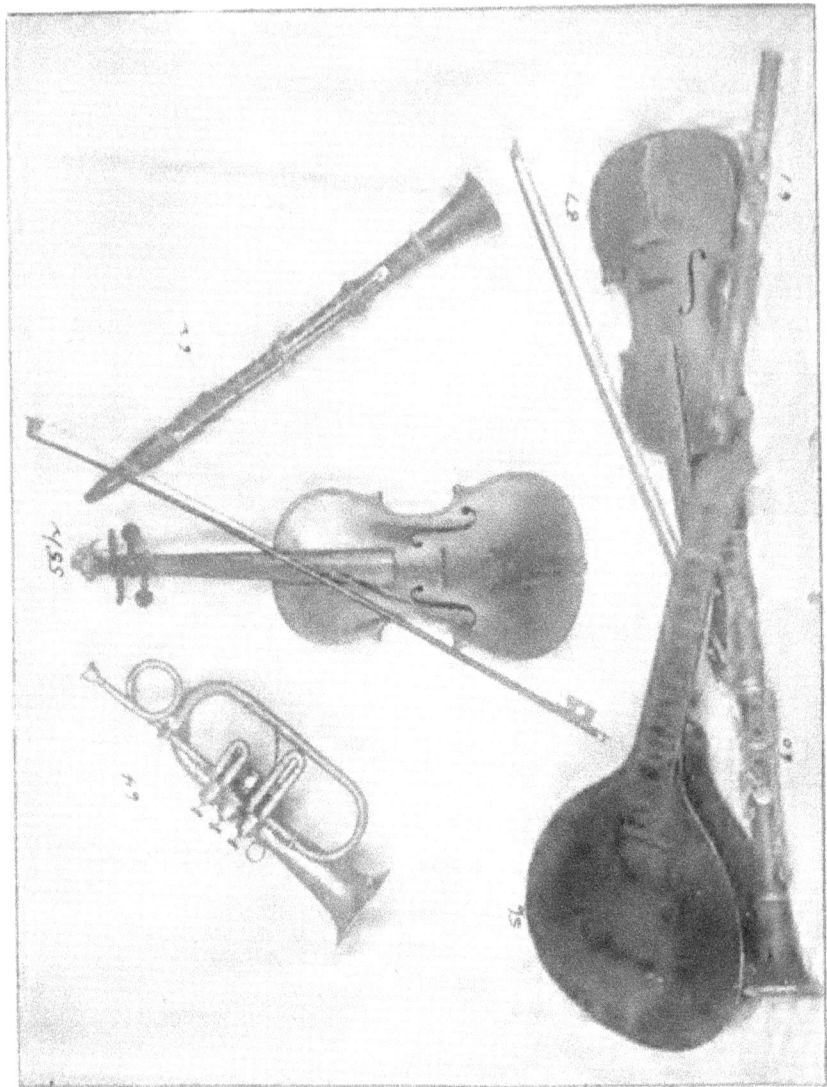

"old models 1892" 65 OLD BRASS CORNET

> This is painted in different positions in several of Mr. Harnett's paintings; also in his last work, "Old Models"

66 OLD BRASS CORNET

> Fine color, and a good model

67 SILVER-PLATED BRASS HORN

> Forming a part of a composition of a large grouping of objects. Painted in Munich, 1884, and sold to a connoisseur in that place

68 PICCOLO

> Painted in the picture exhibited at Cincinnati

MISCELLANEOUS ARTICLES.

Professor's old Frank, 84
my Suns, 1885
69 ROMAN LAMP

> Antique brass. Painted in Mr. Harnett's latest productions

70* ROMAN LAMP

> Antique brass. Painted in the celebrated picture of "Music"; also in the exhibition pictures at Munich, Paris, London and Cincinnati.

Old models 1892
my Suns 1888
Emblems of Peace 89
71* ANTIQUE PITCHER

> Blue-and-white china, with pewter ball top. Painted in Mr. Harnett's pictures, both abroad and in this country; also in his last painting. A favorite model of his

72* CHINA PITCHER

> White; highly glazed blue figures, with name, "O. Rofar." From a collection in Paris Very old

73* CHINA SUGAR BOWL

> Very old English

74 BOHEMIAN VASE

> Decorated with gold

75 * SMALL VASE

> Royal Worcester. Painted in the "Old Cupboard Door"

12

76 TWO-HANDLE MANTEL VASE

Very old and fine French china. Beautifully decorated

77 BRASS EGYPTIAN PITCHER

Fourteenth century. Purchased in Paris. Very rare

78 JAPANESE VASE

79 ENGRAVED GLASS DECANTER

80 STERLING SILVER TANKARD, WITH COVER

Antique, of the fifteenth century; a magnificent piece of early French repoussé work, representing Bacchanalian figures; with coat of arms on the front; bought in Paris at a great expense and used as a model in painting

See plate

81 BRASS CANDLESTICK

Figure, holding receiver. Fifteenth century. Very rare

82 BRASS LAMP

Very old; shape of dragon. Fifteenth century

83 BRONZE FIGURE

Antique, " Bacchus." In the painting of the " Old Cupboard Door," also, in a noted picture sold in London. Very fine and rare

84 BRASS ROMAN LAMP

Antique, with swinging top. Very rare

85 OLD ENGLISH CANDLESTICK

Silver-plated. Part of the composition of the " Old Cupboard "

86 COPPER MEASURE

Two-quart mug, in the composition of the painting owned by Mr. Peter Doomer, of Philadelphia

87 LARGE COPPER TANKARD

Sixteenth century. Very rare

88 COPPER TANKARD PITCHER

Sixteenth century. Rare

89 *PEWTER SERPENTINE TANKARD

Sixteenth century. Fine and rare

? Just Drawn, 11, 90 PEWTER WINE TANKARD

Sixteenth century. With initials K. C. M. on lid, purchased at Stuttgart.

91 STONE PITCHER

With blue marking. Favorite model

92 *OLD STONE BEER MUG

Pewter top

93 ANTIQUE PEWTER BEER MUG

Sixteenth century. Rare

7 Herald '80 94 STONE BEER MUG

"Old Friend." The first model of Mr. Hacuett, and used by him in his smoking compositions

95 CANDELABRA

For three candles. Rigidly ornamented

96 BRASS CANDLESTICK

97 BRASS CANDLESTICK

98 JAPANESE BLUE TEAPOT

99 *CANTON CHINA VASE

Blue decoration. Rare

100 SMALL CLOISONNÉ ENAMELLED VASE

101 BRASS LADLE

Long handle. Very rare and old piece

102 SMALL BRASS CANNON

103 SMALL BRASS CANDLE SNUFFER

Antique. Used in his painting of the "Old Cupboard"

104 SMALL ANTIQUE BRASS CANDLE SNUFFER

105 COPPER JARDINIÈRE
Fine repoussé work. Portrayed in several of Mr. Harnett's paintings

106 BOX OF DRAWING INSTRUMENTS

107 POCKET CIGAR CASE

after Hunt, 85 108 ANTIQUE IRON KEY
Of the Sixteenth century. Painted in Mr. Harnett's famous picture,
" After the Hunt"; also, in "Old Cupboard Door"

109 ROSARY
Very rare. An old Nuremburg rosary, with a small brass cross and
a large one made of wood from Palestine, inlaid with pearl and with
gold-plated caps. Very choice

110 LARGE IVORY CRUCIFIX
This carving, in ivory, of our Saviour crucified, is one of the most
exquisite pieces of ivory carving in this country. Purchased by Mr.
Harnett, at Paris, France, with a view of painting it and then present-
ing the original, together with the picture, to St. Patrick's Cathedral, in New York. Size of figure, twenty inches

111 CRUCIFIX
Antique cross, made of wood from Palestine; bound with brass; inlaid with mother-of-pearl; with bronze figure of the Saviour

112 BRASS FIGURE OF THE CRUCIFIXION

113 IVORY CARVING
Figure of our Saviour; three hundred years old. Bought in Mont
Marte, France

114 OLD CANTON CHINA VASE

115 BRASS CANDLESTICK
Antique figure in armor, holding two receivers. Very rare. Six-
teenth century. Depicted in the painting bought by one of the Royal
Academicians of London

116 POMPEIIAN TABLE LAMP
After the antique

Fig.

117 * BRONZE POMPEIIAN TABLE LAMP
   After the antique

118 PORCELAIN PAINTING
   Beautiful copy of the celebrated painting, " Titian's Will "

119 COPPER WATER KETTLE
   Very old and rare piece, from Frankfort-on-the-Main

120 * REPOUSSÉ BRASS PLACQUE
   Very old and rare.   Allegorical figures.   Depicted in the painting,
   " Ye Knights of Old "

121 * HAMMERED BRASS BOWL
   With figures, in high relief, representing Adam and Eve.   Rare piece
   of repoussé work of the fourteenth century

122 LARGE COPPER WINE COOLER
   Portrayed in a painting sold in Munich, in 1883

123 ANTIQUE BRASS CIGAR TRAY

124 OLD IRON PADLOCK

125 OLD IRON PADLOCK

126 ANTIQUE BRASS TEAKETTLE

127 TERRA-COTTA DECORATED CIGAR HOLDER

128 * ANTIQUE JEWEL CHEST
   Small hand-wrought iron chest, with key.   Dated 1691.   A very cu
   rious piece of open ironwork.   Purchased by Mr. Harnett, in Munich,
   at great expense, and painted in his exhibition picture of 1884.   Sold
   in London

129 * BYZANTINE VASE
   Hammered brass.   Very rare and old.   Representing five religious
   subjects, in high relief

130 BYZANTINE VASE
   Modern facsimile of lot 129

131 ANTIQUE JEWEL CASE
   With engraved glass top.   Initial

132 ANTIQUE BRASS CLOCK
> Sixteenth century. With openwork and engraved brass and steel face

133 MOTHER-OF-PEARL SCENT BOTTLE
> With silver top

134 MOTHER-OF-PEARL CARD CASE

135 ANTIQUE SNUFF BOX
> Made of horn, and bound and studded with German silver. Depicted by Mr. Harnett in several of his famous pictures

136 MOTHER-OF-PEARL SHELL
> Painted in the "Old Cupboard"

137 GOAT-HORN SNUFF BOX
> About two hundred and twenty years old. The name of "Albert Faial" on the top. From the famous collection in Stuttgart

138 ZINC PLATE
> Engraved by William M. Harnett

139 ANOTHER

140 to 143 ENGRAVED COPPER PLATES
> By William M. Harnett

144 MEERSCHAUM PIPE AND COVER
> Presented to Mr. Harnett by Raucher's Verein Club, of Munich, of which he was a member, and used by him as a model

145 LARGE MEERSCHAUM PIPE

146 ANTIQUE WOODEN PIPE
> Carved with coat of arms and initial. From a collection in Stuttgart

147 LARGE MEERSCHAUM PIPE
> Presented to Mr. Harnett by his professor in Munich

148 BRIER-WOOD PIPE

149 ANOTHER

150 MEERSCHAUM PIPE

151 MEERSCHAUM CIGARETTE HOLDER

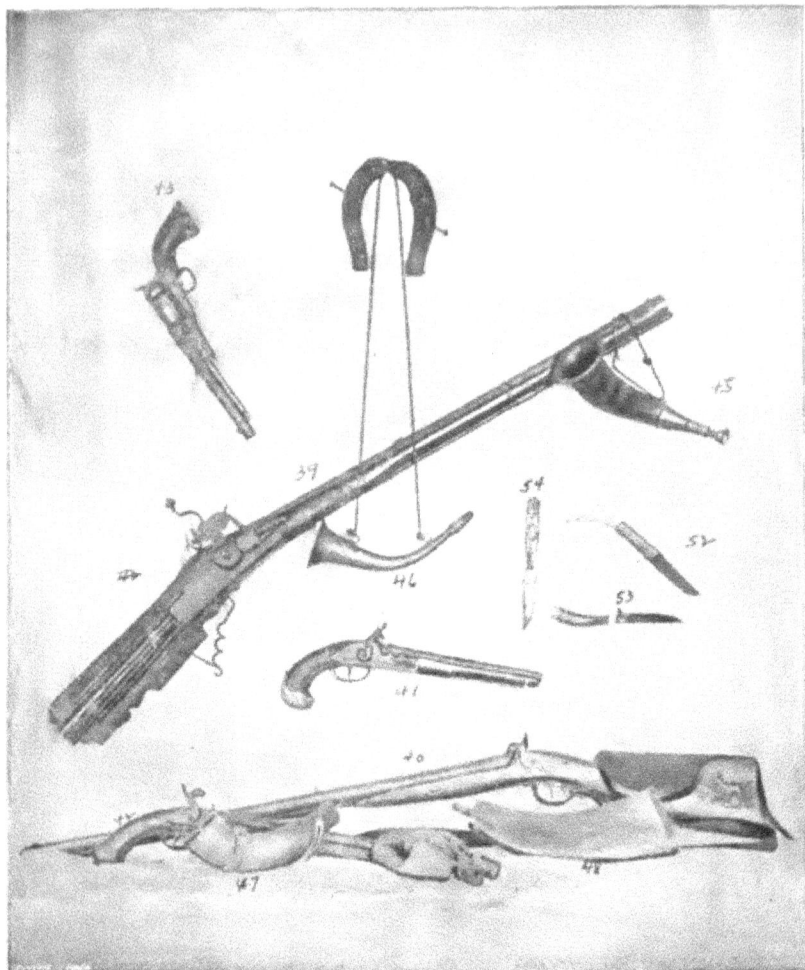

43.   47.   39.   45.
                         46.   54.   52.
           42   41.   48   53.
                         40.

152 LOT PIPE STEMS

153 CLAY PIPE
Smoked by Mr. Harnett, and used as a model for six years in Europe.
Painted in his first smoking composition

154 BOX OF SMOKING TOBACCO

155 DUTCH SNUFFBOX

156 GLASS BOTTLE

after Hunt '85 157 LEATHER POCKET FLASK AND CUP
In the famous painting, " After the Hunt "

158 STONE CORDIAL BOTTLE

159 WINE BOTTLE, COVERED WITH STRAW
One of Mr. Harnett's first models, and introduced in all his first compositions

160 OLD BLACK BOTTLE, WITH RED SEAL
One of Mr. Harnett's first models

161 TWO OLD ENGLISH STONE BOTTLES
Hand-painted

162 ANTIQUE BRASS LAMP

163 and 164 TWO GINGER JARS
Used by Mr. Harnett in many of his paintings

165 OLD LEATHER HUNTING BAG
From Munich, and painted in the noted picture, " After the Hunt "

166 OLD LEATHER GAME BAG, LACE COVER
Purchased at Frankfort-on-the-Main

167 COPPER PANEL OF JOAN OF ARC
In high relief. Model, by G. Faraoni. Plush frame

168 SAME IN STEEL
Walnut frame

169 to 174 LONDON HORSE-SHOES

175 MR. HARNETT'S WORKING EASEL.

176 MR. HARNETT'S PALETTE

Purchased by him on his last visit to Munich, and used by him until his death

176½ MR. HARNETT'S SCHOOL SLATE

The slate used by Wm. M. Harnett during his school boy days at the "Zane Street" school; upon which he has drawn four groupings of Still Life; dated 1861. This is probably his first attempt. The slate was found among the effects of his mother, after her death.

177 MR. HARNETT'S MAUL-STICK

178 MR. HARNETT'S PAINTING STAND

179 MR. HARNETT'S PAINTING COAT

180 MR. HARNETT'S STUDIO CAP

181 FELT HAT

Painted by Mr. Harnett, in the painting "After the Hunt"

182 MR. HARNETT'S PAINTING JACKET

183 ANOTHER

184 SMALL JACKET

185 WOOD CARVING

The Holy Family. An exquisite piece of work of the fifteenth century. Very rare

186 LEAD-PENCIL DRAWING

Female figure

187 LEAD-PENCIL DRAWING

Gladiator

188 LEAD-PENCIL DRAWING

Male figure

189 LEAD-PENCIL AND COLOR DRAWING

Boy, whittling

190 LEAD-PENCIL DRAWING

Male figure

191 LEAD-PENCIL DRAWING

Female head

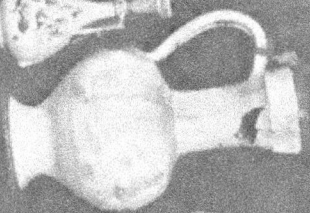

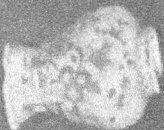

73   72   75   71   76   99   114

192 LEAD-PENCIL DRAWING
    Female figure

193 CHARCOAL DRAWING
    Female figure   .

194 LEAD-PENCIL DRAWING
    Old man's head

195 CHARCOAL DRAWING
    Female figure

196 LEAD-PENCIL DRAWING
    Male figure

197 LEAD-PENCIL DRAWING
    Old beer man

198 LEAD-PENCIL DRAWING
    Design for church window

199 SKETCH, IN COLORS
    Female figure

200 LEAD-PENCIL DRAWING
    Female figure

201 LEAD-PENCIL SKETCH
    Female figure

202 INK DRAWING
    Dead bird

203 LEAD-PENCIL DRAWING
    Male figure

204 CHARCOAL SKETCH
    Male figure

205 SMALL STILL-LIFE, IN CHARCOAL
    With design for window, which was exhibited and sold in the Academy in Munich

206 INK DRAWING
    Dead bird

207 CHARCOAL SKETCH
Female figure

208 TWO CARDS OF FANCY INITIALS, IN COLORS

209 to 219 ELEVEN WINDSOR AND NEWTON'S PRE-
PARED MAHOGANY PANELS. Various sizes

220 to 234 FIFTEEN PREPARED CANVASES. Various
sizes

235 UNFINISHED PICTURE, ON CANVAS

236 PIECE OF CANVAS, 1½ x 1⅛ yards

237 PIECE OF CANVAS, 3½ x 1¼ yards

238 LOT BACKGROUND CLOTH

239 PIECE OF CANVAS, 23 x 33 inches

240 OLD HOUSE: Fourth and Locust streets
Painted by Mr. Harnett, 1877, looking from his studio

241 THREE PIECES CANVAS, different sizes

242 LARGE RULER

243 TWO " T " SQUARES

244 PAINT CASE

245 GERMAN BUCKSKIN SHOT-POUCH

246 LOT OLD MODELS

247 BAMBOO FISHING ROD

248 FIVE FELT HATS, assorted
Used as models

249 LARGE IRON CHAIN

250 THREE PIECES GLASSWARE

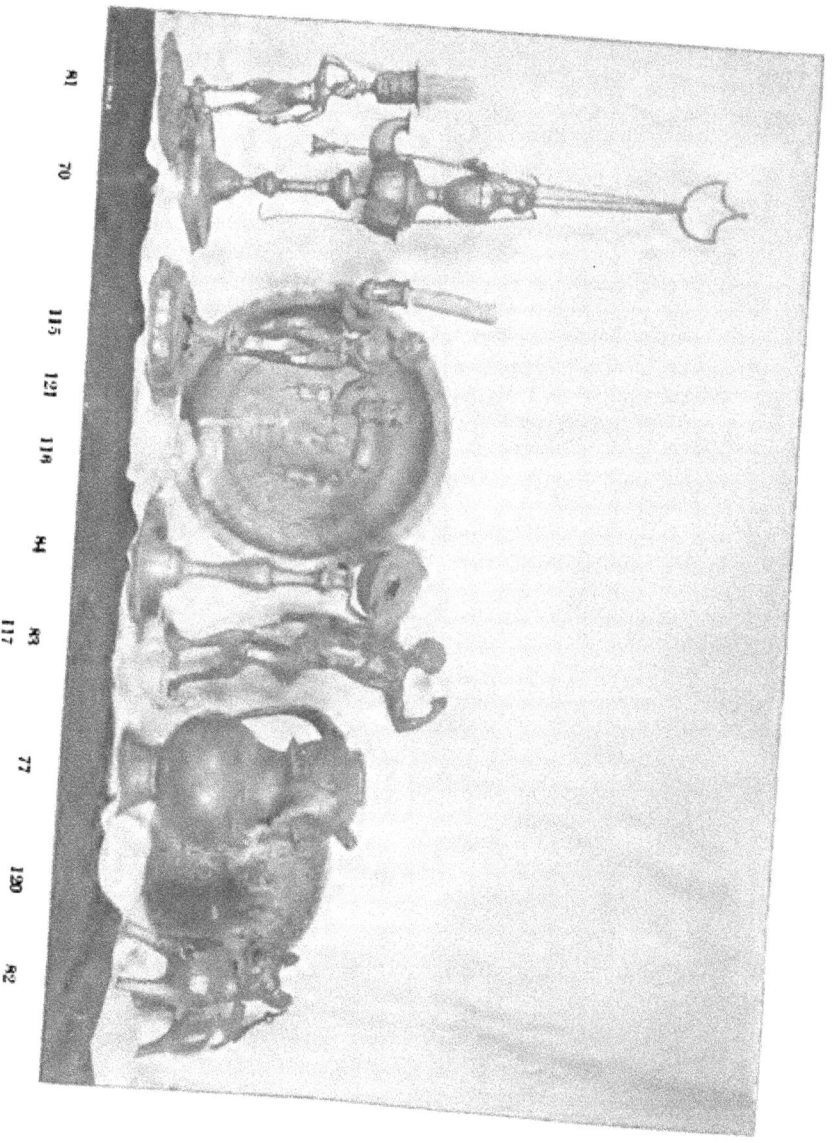

81 70 115 121 118 84 83 77 120 82
117

251 LOT ORIGINAL DESIGNS FOR SILVER SPOONS
Drawn by Mr. Harnett

252 LOT MODELS

253 LOT OLD RUSTY IRON HINGES, ESCUTCHEONS, ETC.
Used as models in door pictures

254 WALNUT SKETCH BOX

255 TIN SKETCH BOX

256 LARGE WALNUT PAINT-BOX AND PAINTS
The one used by Mr. Harnett all through Europe, and filled with assorted tube colors

256A LARGE BLENDER

256B LOT BRUSHES

256C LOT BRUSHES

256D LOT BRUSHES

256E LOT BRUSHES

256F LOT BRUSHES

256G LOT BRUSHES

256H LOT BRUSHES

256J LOT PALETTE KNIVES, ETC.

256K EBONY PARALLEL RULER

256L VARNISH BRUSH

257 to 281 TWENTY-FIVE PHOTOGRAPHS, INTERIORS, EXTERIORS, ETC

282 to 301 TWENTY PHOTOGRAPHS, FIGURES, INTERIORS, ETC.

302 CINCINNATI ENQUIRER
This was painted in a picture ordered by Joseph P. Abbe, of Holyoke, Mass., for which he gave $5000, and is as represented. Burnt

303 PIECE OF MUSIC "Melodies"
Painted in Mr. Harnett's last picture

304 to 313 TEN LOTS SHEET MUSIC
Used as models by Mr. Harnett in many of his noted paintings

314 PORTFOLIO, WITH PRINTED DESIGNS

315 PORTFOLIO, WITH PRINTED DESIGNS

316 ANTIQUE RUSSIAN BRASS COFFEE URN

317 BRASS CALL BELL

318 LOT ARTIFICIAL FLOWERS AND GRAPES

319 COCOANUT
Used as a model by Mr. Harnett in his paintings

320 FIVE BONE GUITAR KEYS

321 TIN SIGN

322 STUDENT'S LAMP, BRASS

323 STUDENT'S LAMP, BRASS

324 LOT CIGAR BOXES
Used as models by Mr. Harnett in his celebrated pictures

325 OLD WOODEN DOOR
The background used in the celebrated painting, " After the Hunt '

326 GREEN DOOR
Used as a model by Mr. Harnett in many of his celebrated paintings

327 FELT-COVERED DOOR
Used as a model

328 OLD-GOLD VELVET EMBROIDERED COVER

329 ANTIQUE TAPESTRY COVER

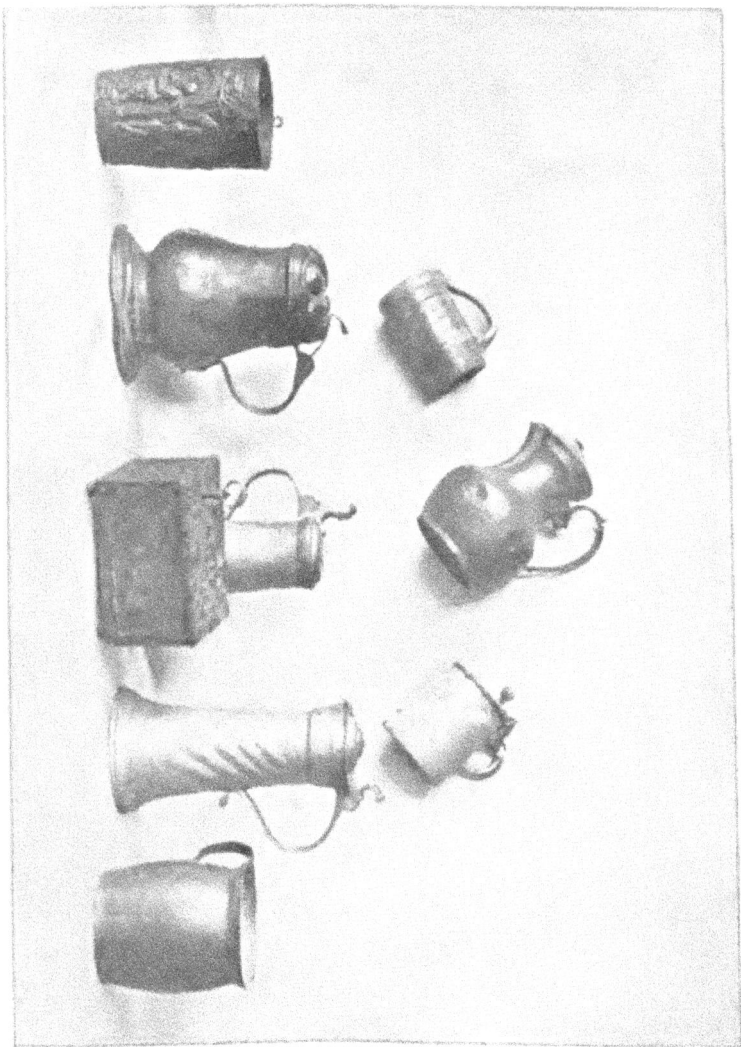

330 ONE AND ONE-EIGHTH YARDS OLD-GOLD SILK

331 ANTIQUE TAPESTRY COVER

332 ANTIQUE TURKISH RUG
Painted in the celebrated picture " Music "

333 ONE AND FIVE-EIGHTHS YARDS FIGURED VELOUR TAPESTRY

334 EMBROIDERED RUG

335 JAPANESE PORTIÈRE

336 ONE AND THREE-EIGHTHS YARDS EMBROID-ERED CASHMERE

337 FRENCH PLUSH BORDERED COVER

338 ONE AND THREE-EIGHTHS YARDS FIGURED TAPESTRY

339 ANTIQUE TURKISH RUG

340 ONE AND THREE-EIGHTHS YARDS VELOUR

341 to 374 THIRTY-FOUR PIECES OF DRAPERY
Used by Mr. Harnett in his various paintings

375 to 379 FIVE PIECES VELVET DRAPERY

380 to 382 THREE PIECES MOHAIR DRAPERY

383 and 384 TWO TABLE COVERS

BOOKS.

385 Munster Sebastian Cosmography. Illustrated with curious old maps and woodcuts. Folio, embossed hog-skin, with brass corners.
One of Mr. Harnett's famous models

386 Roman Missal. In black and red. Illustrated. Folio, old calf. Monachii, 1680

387 Maximilian's Code of Laws. In German and Latin. Folio, embossed hogskin. Munich, 1756

388 Vallensis Andrie. Juris Canonici. 4to, embossed hogskin. Coloniæ, 1651

389 **Hogarth,** William. Works of. Reproduced in outline, with text in German. Royal 8vo, half calf. Stuttgart, 1840

390 **Becker's** Ornamental Penmanship.

391 Old Latin **Book.** Bound in vellum.
A favorite model

392 Weixer, J. C. Dissertationus in Priviligia Statuum Provincialium. Quarto, old calf. Munich, 1719

393 Don Quixote. In Spanish. Illustrated with curious old woodcuts. 2 vols. 4to, vellum. Madrid, 1750

394 Justinian's Code. In Latin.
A favorite old model

395 St. Chrysostom's Commentary on the New Testament. 8vo, embossed hogskin. Antwerpt, 1544

396 Mylius Malerische Fuszreise. 8vo, half calf. Carlsruc, 1818

397 Flowers of the Illustrious Poets. In Latin. Small 8vo, old calf. Argentorari, 1549

398 Zwingern, Geweissenhaffte Apothecar. 8vo, embossed vellum. Nuremberg, 1721

399 Morgan, Lady. Florence McCarthy. 8vo, cloth.

400 Maxæmyliani Vrienti Gaudensis Epigrammatum. 12mo, vellum. Antverpiæ, 1603

401 Schutz's Compendium Juris. 12mo, vellum.

402 Bruelis Gualtri. Medicinæ Theorica et Empirica 12mo, vellum. Lugduni, 1647

403 Dummy book.
Used as a model

404 Map of Paris.

405 to 414 10 lots of old books.
Used as models

415–416 Lot of pamphlets.

417 Novel.
With lead-pencil sketch on last page

418 Trunk.

419 Trunk.

THOMAS BIRCH & SONS, Auctioneers.